As The Earth Lies Still

As The Earth Lies Still

poems

J. M. Oak

ISBN: 979-8-218-38013-7

for Craig, forever my Sun on a cloudy day

A note on the cover art —

When I was sixteen, I drew a pencil drawing very similar to the image on the cover while in the worst depressive episode of my life. The original drawing has been lost to time, but I did my best to recreate it. The hand is meant to be a representation of my depression, holding the world in its grasp. "As The Earth Lies Still" does not intend to celebrate nor glorify mental illness.

J. M. Oak

According to the DSM-5[1], *mania* is "a distinct period of abnormally and persistently elevated, expansive, or irritable mood and abnormally and persistently goal-directed behavior or energy, lasting at least one week and present most of the day, nearly every day (or any duration if hospitalization is necessary)."

---

[1] American Psychiatric Association. (2013). *Diagnostic and statistical manual of mental disorders* (5th ed.).

Part I

Summer

It

"It" is an ugly, dark thing that lurks in the shadows
of my brain, waiting in the wings to pounce like a
prowling panther, dangerous and deadly.

"It" thirsts for my blood and my sanity, a parasitic
entity twirling its black tendrils around my brain,
working its way into my veins, making my blood boil.

"It" takes over if I let It, roaring anger escaping
my lips, hellfire filling my body from head to toe,
heat searing my brain, all with a smile plastered on.

"It" whispers wonders in my ear, promising me
glory, fame, and fortune. It weaves webs of lies
and tells me I have powers I do not possess, malicious.

"It" most certainly wishes me dead
and would kill me if I let It, pulling at my strings
and forcing me into treacherous situations without remorse.

"It" fills me with euphoria, energy, and excitement.
It tells me that It knows what is best for me,
if only I would allow It to take over. I must not. I will not.

"It" is not me, I am not It. It is mania, a mental illness that I have lived with
since I was born one spring day in May. It is currently lurking.
I see and feel It.

"It" is tamed by lithium, heavy metal balancing the chemicals in my brain,
and a mood stabilizer, calming me and unraveling Its glorious falsehoods.
"It" is not me, I am not it. I must control It, or It will control me.

I will not let "It" ruin my life,
It is not worthy of such a beautiful thing.
My life is mine.

Evil

It most certainly should be described as evil,
vile, twisted, ugly, wicked, hateful, and dark.
It maintains that It is good, however, smiling at me.

Well, more like baring Its teeth like a rabid animal,
a sick mockery of a warm smile. Again, It is wholly evil.
It doesn't know any other way to be. It was born from hate.

Wrapping Its tentacles around my brain like a Kraken,
It squeezes the mental stability from the grey matter, refusing to let
go. Evil is often disguised as good, but one must remain vigilant.

I can always feel It lurking in the background, a shadowy
form that slithers and stalks Its prey — me. It shifts shapes,
sometimes a viper, quick and deadly, sometimes a panther,
prowling and vicious.

I am equipped to deal with all of these forms, choosing from my
arsenal of weapons to match whatever form It takes. Therapy and
meds make up the bulk of my weaponry, but I also have other
warriors who fight by my side.

Evil is no match for us.

Its Anger

Its anger bubbles up inside my insides like bile.
Hot, thick, and dark as Hell, burning my throat,
It tastes like poison, like acid, like something Evil.

Everyone should clear the room, quick —
a bomb is ticking down, a nuclear blast looms.
My voice is full of hate and malice. Venom drips from my lips.

I lick the corner of my mouth, only encouraging
It to raise my voice even louder, full of bass and booming,
I can't control It, though I try and try.

Tidal wave after tidal wave of searing hot anger
washes over me, I become feverish and burn up.
It takes over, I dissociate to escape Its wrath.

I feel like a monster, people run and hide from me,
grabbing pitchforks and torches, shouting back in
defense. They are no match for It. I alone must stop It.

I force my hand down Its gaping maw,
shoving the dark matter down, down, down Its esophagus,
back from whence it came. The thick black liquid burns my hand

and forearm, but I mustn't stop. It is not done with me yet.
I finally force the black, tar-like substance down far enough,
clamping Its mouth shut, tying a cord of calm

around Its snout. I breathe a sigh of relief
and wipe the venom from my lips, preparing myself
for the next bout with It.

Pendulum

Everyone in my life is so tired of "It"
and trust me, I am too. I am tired of being up,
up early in the morning, mood up, Sun's up.

I am tired of being on the upswing, on this fucking
pendulum I am doomed to ride forever and always.
Up, up, up, I swing up and haven't come down

for a few weeks now. I am dizzy from the altitude,
my ears ringing and my clothes sopping wet from
being in the clouds for, what, twenty days? More?

I'm afraid of freefalling, however, I am afraid of the
pendulum thread snapping, sending me spiraling down
into the roiling dark ocean of depression that threatens to swallow me.

I want to get off this swing, it isn't fun anymore.
It never was. The ocean below is so deep, so so so fucking deep.
The water is freezing and unseen things grab my legs, trying to pull me

down, down, down into depression. I don't wanna sink. Please don't let
me sink. I'm not even on fucking antidepressants anymore, I can't even
take them because they can make mania worse. What a joke, right?
How do I swing without swinging too high?

How do I swing on this swing without the thread snapping, sending
me spiraling? How do I live with this damn disease that rots my brain?
I want to get off this pendulum.

Mad Hatter

Welcome to the tea party, love. Pull up a chair and
stay a while, won't you? I am the Mad Hatter,
but we're all a little mad down here in Wonderland.

I mean no harm, I swear it, but this poison has seeped
from my hat into my brain and it has made
me a bit mad, a bit loony, a bit manic —

Why don't you take that hat off, Hatter? Well, you see,
the hat has attached itself to my head, and thus I am
doomed to wear the poison thing forever.

It's not all bad, though. People love my hat!
I don't, however. The poison makes my head ache
and my heart has turned to stone.

Anyways, have some tea
before it gets cold, my love.

The Angry Man In My House

Sometimes, most times, I'd wager, I am the angry
man in my house. But sometimes I am just the sad,
scared little boy who is the outlet for the angry man's anger.

Neither feel good. Both, in fact, are downright terrible.
Both the angry man and the scared boy are victims of the same
emotion, but neither know this. There is just the fiery anger and the
shivering fear.

I don't want to be the angry man or the scared boy,
I want to be a ray of sunshine, a beacon of peace,
a harbinger of joy.

I can do this if I try, I know it. I must.

The Dragonfly and the Bat

I had a dream last night where I was a beautiful green dragonfly
with sparkling, iridescent wings and a fluttering heartbeat.
I was buzzing through the clouds, carefree, happy, alive.

All of a sudden, out of the corner of my eye, I spotted a huge black bat
with leathery wings, huge teeth, beady dark eyes, and a savage thirst for
blood. Mine. It saw me and instantly zeroed in,

zooming towards me in the sky, literally a bat out of Hell. I zipped away,
flying as fast as my thin wings would carry me, desperately trying to
avoid becoming prey. It screeched, a bloodthirsty

demonic sound, and I knew it was coming. I was ready, though. I'm
smarter and craftier than some bat and I refuse to be its victim this time. I
am in control and I will get away, I just have to keep

flying towards the Sun.

The Thread

I woke up this morning with salt water in my lungs, drowning
choking, sputtering, trying to expel the icy ocean water from
my insides, the frigid waters of depression already consuming me.

The pendulum thread must have snapped last night as I slept.
I was not ready for the chill of the ocean, I was flying just yesterday —
hitting the water after a long flight is never easy and I was not prepared.

The water surrounds me, no shoreline can be seen. All I see is grey,
all I feel is exhaustion and numbness. The manic euphoria has vanished
overnight, the fire inside me snuffed out by this endless grey sea.

The Beast that was tearing apart my insides now drowns besides me,
gurgling on grey ocean water. I am a better swimmer, however, the Beast
has not learned how to stay afloat while depressed, as I have.

Gritting my teeth and setting my jaw, I start to kick my legs.
I am not trying to reach the horizon in hopes of finding the shore —
there is not one. I simply must tread water, stay afloat, not let it kill me,
as I always have, as I always will.

I will live in this ocean for the rest of eternity, as the battle with
depression is never truly won. It simply is. I am damn good
at treading water and I will not drown. I will be strong.

The thread may have snapped, but my resolve has not.

Phaethon

Have you ever heard the story of Phaethon,
Son of the Sun, Helios? He was spurned by
his father, who had ignored him his whole life.

In retribution, Phaethon asked his father if he
could drive the Sun Chariot across the sky one
summer morning to prove that he was truly, indelibly

Son of the Sun. His father immediately denied his
request, warning him of the danger and the fiery
nature of the team of horses that pulled the Chariot.

Phaethon insisted however, he desired to prove his
worth to his father and to the rest of the world. Helios
finally agreed after much hesitation. Sadly, this would lead to

Phaethon's untimely death. He lost control of the horses
while flying over a pine forest, burning the entire sea of trees
to grey ash. He dried up oceans and lit cities on fire, pride

and arrogance proving to be his undoing. Eventually, Phaethon
too burned, turned to ash and bone by the horses' fire. He hurtled
through the air, freefalling, hitting the ground with a soft thud.

I too feel as though I am in freefall, the manic energy no longer
setting fire to my organs and brain. I too am ash, grey specks
of nothing, weightless, fragile, able to be blown away by

the slightest breeze. I am thankful to be ash, however. I would
rather be nothing than burn any more bridges, I would rather be
nothing than destroy any more relationships, I would rather be

ashen, grey, and depressed than manic. Nothing is hotter than
manic rage, and my insides were burning up. I was tired of being
on fire and so I am thankful to be ash. I finally am free, riding the

zephyrous wind to freedom, free from the fire, thank the gods.

Sunbaked Melancholy

July has been a rough month so far, with long hot
days filled with malaise. Winter is difficult, but the cold
gloom has nothing on sunbaked melancholy.

Lounging on a pool raft, lazily floating atop the cool, still water,
I should be smiling in the warmth of the Sun.
Instead, I scowl and squint, cursing the

red glow of my pale skin, the sweat beading on my forehead,
and the profound emptiness in my soul. Not a cloud in the sky,
but my heart is shadowed by a black storm,

torrential downpour is inevitable. I want to enjoy the Sun
and the buzz of the cicadas, I do, but I cannot shake
this sunbaked melancholy.

Zombie

Dying is for the living. It has always been this way.
Zombies, however, in their state of reanimation, are an anomaly, like me. What does it mean to truly live? As the biological clock ticks ever forward, how do we make the most of those ticks?

I am fascinated by the concept of "zombie," corpses that stalk the Earth, unsatisfied with the amount of ticks they were given. Lost. Or maybe they were brought back to life by necromancy, magicked

back from beyond into the land of the living, given one more chance at this thing called life. What does it mean to be immortal? What if the zombie's head is never removed and thrown into the fire? What if a stake is never driven through their heart? What happens then? Where do they wander? Where do they go?

The Egyptians had their mummies, dead mommies and daddies and brothers and sisters and cousins and grandmothers. The Inca peoples were embalmed and preserved too. Why? Why can we not let the dead lie? Why can we not let them rest?

If man is so cruel, I hope death is kinder.
Let me rest please.
I deserve it.

Worry

Worry is a worm eating away at the insides
of an apple, coring it from the middle outwards.
Worrying can be a good thing, of course. It keeps us

alive, it keeps us from danger. But what happens
when worry eats the apple whole, leaving nothing
but the core and stem? Nothing left in worry's wake

but trash. You have to leave some of the apple,
you see. Don't let worry eat you alive, love, save
some of your flesh and juice for yourself.

The Beast

My therapist once told me it could be helpful to imagine
my depression as a physical entity and not just a conglomeration
of darkness, so I have decided to name my depression the Beast.

The Beast resembles a wolf-like creature with blood-stained fur as
black as pitch, staring back at me with cold, unfeeling eyes. The
Beast is monstrous and huge, a hulking, evil thing with claws

that could easily rip through flesh, my flesh, without remorse.
The Beast's claws are long and black to match its fur, so sharp they
almost glint in the light. Its gnarled paws are enormous, twisted,

grasping, with long toes and pulsing veins. The Beast, of course,
has its teeth as well, rows and rows of sharp teeth that want
nothing more than to tear me apart. The Beast is always

bloodthirsty and hungry, feeding on my pain and suffering, my
struggle strengthening it. I have known the Beast for over a decade
now and I do not think it ever plans on letting me go.

Thus, I am destined to combat the Beast until the end of time,
an everlong fight to the death. Claws and teeth clashing against
prescriptions and gumption.

Who shall win?

The Beast and I

The Beast and I dance in the dark each night, a slow, mournful
waltz under the glow of the Moon. We make a great pair,
the Beast and I, the oldest of confidants.

The Beast has danced with me for years, since I was a boy, as I
mentioned earlier, so we know each other well. The Beast and I
dance in the dark each night as I try to ignore the searing pain

of claws digging into my arm, the Beast's reminder that it has no
plans of letting me go. I have accepted this. I know the Beast and I
will dance in the dark under the glow of the Moon for many years

to come, so I best practice my footwork,
in case we dance forever.

The Moon

The moon is full tonight and I yearn to bathe
in its soft light, gorgeous waterfalls of white
cascading down in glorious waves, enveloping.

The moonlight shines over the grey ocean
that threatens to drown me, the grey ocean
that I call home. "The Moon controls the tides,"

I remind myself, allowing a sigh of relief.
The Moon surely will not let me drown,
all I must do is keep treading water.

August Blues

It seems as if I have a serious case of the August Blues,
a seemingly misplaced depression in the warmth of late summer,
where the Sun shines long and the birds chirp in the morning.

However, that sunshine casts a long shadow and my fight with the Beast continues. It snarls and snaps its incisors, hungry, twisted, and ravenous. I refuse to be a victim, though.

The Beast and I dance our age old dance, fighting and flowing our way through the motions. It has gotten old, however, and you are tired of the same moves, made worse in the Sun. And so, time moves ever forward,

and my dance with the Beast continues evermore, until the end of time, through each and every season that was or will be.

Uncharted Waters

Beyond what man can see
there lie wild, uncharted waters,
roiling and dark, deep and mysterious
where sirens sing their siren songs, luring
unsuspecting sailors to their ruin.

I am one of these sailors, sailing on these wild,
uncharted waters of sobriety and mental stability
thanks to my meds, therapy, doctors, and support network.
However, the siren's haunting song of addiction still resonates
in my ears, calling out to me, a melody that promises dopamine
and serotonin.

Weed and wine were always my downfall, ushering
in a manic episode that ripped the very fabric of my life to shreds
as the sirens laughed. I am happy to be free of the vice grip of
these vices. I am afraid, but I know I can go the distance and
conquer these wild, uncharted waters that sailors fear.

Part II

Fall

The Fog

Wandering through this dense grey Fog, I wonder
if the Beast is lurking somewhere, waiting for the
perfect moment to ambush me, catching me

with my guard down. I stumble over something,
eyes still having not adjusted to the murky cloudiness.
Somewhere, somewhere far away, I hear a growl.

The Beast has caught my scent and has begun to stalk me
in the dark. This Fog is its home. The Beast has a distinct
advantage and will surely find me. I pick up my pace,

hustling through the Fog, trying to keep my labored breathing as
quiet as possible. I panic and start to sprint as I hear the pounding
of paws behind me, sharp nails scratching stone, the foul smelling

breath of the Beast somehow cutting through the clouds.
I close my eyes briefly, praying to whoever will listen.
I grit my teeth, set my face, and refuse to let it catch me.

Porcelain

I have always said that I have thick skin.
In reality, my skin is not thick, it is hard.
Pale and thin, like porcelain,

I sometimes feel as though I will shatter
at the slightest touch, a shift in the breeze
threatens to break me.

I am not a diamond in the rough,
I am the rough, the strong, and the brittle.
I am porcelain.

Made of Stone

When I was young, I would skip alongside the creek
collecting rocks and stones, not knowing that someday,
I would be one too. A Rock that would not give nor break

nor crack no matter the size of the burden placed upon it.
One day, however, a splintery fracture appeared on the Rock's side.
"It's nothing," the Rock pants and grunts, feeling the strain for the first time.

Over time, the Rock continued to strain. Those around him tried to fill the cracks with gold, like a vase, lustrous and shining. Gold could not save the Rock, as it was not a vase. The gold began to slowly melt in the hot Sun, and soon, the Rock broke once and for all, pieces

of stone crumbling to the ground. Years later, a man came upon all of the broken pieces of the Rock. Dusting off one small piece, his brow furrowed in confusion. "What happened here?" He wondered to himself,

looking around at the broken pieces, a soul turned to gravel, a humongous jigsaw of a puzzle. The man was clever, however. He slowly put the stone back together, building a pillar that reached towards the sky, stronger, more stable, more able to weather the storm.

Painting Flowers

I will paint these flowers for you until the end of time,
even if I think the task is arduous and sometimes even
a bit silly, as the rain will always wash away the paint.

I've shown you all of my cards and gave you my heart.
I am overjoyed to be in your garden,
painting these flowers for you.

Stumbling down that rabbit hole into this Wonderland
with you will always and forever be the best thing that has
ever happened to me. Sometimes, I just wish that my red paint

was good enough for you, that my art and hard work were seen
and appreciated. I don't want to lose my head, Your Grace, I just
want to continue painting these flowers for you until the end

of days, even as I watch the rain wash the red away.

He Just Doesn't Get It

I know he loves me more than life itself, but unfortunately,
he just doesn't get it. He doesn't. I hope he never will understand
what it's like to live with depression. He just doesn't understand

what it's like to live in a world shaded in greyscale, to walk through life
with apathy, to look in the mirror with hate in your heart, to rot in bed
on a Sunday, to drown in the endless dark sea. He just doesn't understand

what it's like to yearn for a fraction of joy, to force every smile, to feel
the lead in your legs, to wish for a deathlike sleep that never comes.
He just doesn't understand what it's like to fantasize about disappearing,

to want to sink into the ground, to want to let the Earth consume you.
I know he loves me more than life, but, unfortunately, he just doesn't get
it and I hope he never will. I want him to continue to shine, to be the light

in my life while I wallow in the dark. He wants to fix me, but I am not
broken. He wants to fix me with "sleeping better" and "walks in the Sun"
and "positive self talk." He wants to fix something he does not

understand, and is thus doomed to fail. He doesn't understand that this is
something I must live with, a forever thing that I must shape myself
around, because the Beast is here to stay. I can muzzle and tranquilize

and placate, but it will never leave me completely, my faithful
companion, my oldest friend. The Beast lays at my side, quiet now.

Dawn

Dawn's light brings new hope of a bright and happy morning. You look in the fridge for breakfast, remember the bagels you bought yesterday, and allow yourself a small smile. It works though, it cracks the stony exterior that the Beast so carefully chisels to perfection

over your skull, your brain encased in black granite. The gentle call of lovebirds wins you another small smile, this one a bit bigger. The world is full of small wonders that allow for, no, encourage smiles big and small. The Sun peeks over the overcast gloom, casting warm light

on your face from the living room window whose glow is loved by both you and your plants. Dawn's light brings hope of a bright and happy morning, Sunday, to be specific.

A third smile starts —

Dusk

When day turns slowly and lazily into night,
the moment I realize that dusk is approaching,
the Beast perks up its ears and licks its chops,

ready to feed, ready for a taste of the profound emptiness inside,
the endless nothing that somehow fills me up. The Beast feasts on
melancholy and malaise, it hungers for nothing, ravenously filling

its belly with the sadness that threatens to consume me. I try to
muzzle it as I don't want it to take another bite from the slim
pickings of my heart. It is more powerful at night.

Most times I am helpless. I simply lie there, listening
to the sickening sounds of its jaws smacking together,
gleefully relishing in my pain. I sigh, a deep hearty sigh,
and wait for first light.

Claw Marks

My eyes well with tears at the thought of all the beings that have
left me. First, my childhood dog, Trooper, whom I mourned alone
sitting in the parking lot of a strip mall near my mom's house.
Huge hot tears rolled down my face, sobbing.

I didn't get to say goodbye.

Second, my dad, who was never really present anyway.
His passing was slow and quiet, fading into nonexistence
with the ease of a soft sigh.

He didn't deserve a goodbye.

Finally, my gram, the matriarchal rock
holding our family on her shoulders,
crumbling as she died.

I said goodbye but it didn't make it easier.

I screamed and wept and clawed and fought, but it won't bring
them back. Their passing long in the past, but tonight is when I cry,
thinking of claw marks on the dead and gone.

Dead of Night

I wake up in the dead of night when everything is
still and unmoving. Witching hour, not a stir, except
for the chill of the breeze that comes in through the

crack in the bedroom window. Your mind goes to a dark place
as you toss and turn, trying to find your place in the silent
darkness.

Birds sleeping, the world turns slowly in the dead of night.
You shut your eyes once more, hoping to find some peace
in the inky solitude, hoping to find yourself in the dark.

Smoke

As I wipe the last few tears from my face,
I notice the smell of old Marlboro smoke lingering on my
fingers, a stale smell that only serves to remind me

the thick clouds of smoke I choke into my lungs will
not fill the emptiness I feel inside. I light up another
in the cold autumn monotony,

hoping that this one will be different. It will not.
“Those things will kill you!” I hear my mom’s voice in my head.
“Good,” I think as I inhale again.

That Lavender Bedroom

We fell in love in that lavender bedroom, only big
enough for a queen sized bed and my beloved
bookshelf, full of fantasy that we bonded over,

both voracious and avid devourers of anything
magical, anything surreal, anything to let us escape
the harshness of our realities. Then, we found

each other, and everything changed. Our lives
became one on that brisk day on the top
of a mountain, shouting our love

to the heavens, hoping the gods were listening.
We fell in love in that lavender bedroom
and I would not have it any other way.

The Moon II

The Moon shines brightest upon those thrust into the deepest dark, guiding those befallen ones into Her Light, pure and clear. Her brilliance contends with that of the Sun, yet moonlight does not scorch or burn, it embraces.

Shine on, O Moon, shine your light upon me so that I may escape the darkness behind my eyes, the darkness that threatens to swallow me whole. I cannot see, O Moon, I am flying blind in the dark with nothing but wit and grit to guide me, doomed to crash.

The Oak Tree

Over the years, I have grown hard due to all of the
hardship and misery. A thick outer bark has formed, rough
to the touch, like sandpaper. However, I am not hard to the core,

like stone, I am soft on the inside, vulnerable and silky.
Despite my bark, despite the struggle, I grow stronger each and
every day, a pillar of strength to stand the test of time for
generations to come.

My leaves are green
and full, as is my heart.
I am an oak, standing tall.

Dampened

I am not allowed to feel too excited, too much joy,
elation, or freedom. I wanted to listen to music tonight,
but I was told that was an "absolute no"

because music could trigger an episode. I felt a wave
of anger swell up inside me, sloshing back and forth
in my belly, hot and vile, ready to erupt.

I hate when my flame is dampened, my joy squashed
like a bug under a shoe, smeared into the pavement,
staining it red and bright. Chained to the ground with my

wings clipped, I am trapped in this earthly realm
that cannot contain the wholeness of my soul.
My fire burns bright still.

Comfort

Comfort can be more than a feeling if you let it.
Comfort can become a place, curled up with a cat on your lap
on your tattered grey couch, warm and content.

Comfort can be a person, the one you want to wrap your arms
around at the end of a long day, feeling safe and secure in their
warmth. Comfort can be anything you want it to be.

Me? For me, comfort is the smell of old book pages,
flickering candles, and being hand in hand
with my one true love.

Home Sweet Home

They say "home" is where the heart is, and baby,
mine's with you. Home is not home unless you are there,
sharing the space we created, together.

Home is no longer a red brick house on the hill, but a stately,
charming, and handsome building near the river. Home is
apartment two, home is with you. Home is where we make crab
rangoon puffs, home is where we trim the kitty's nails

together, home is where we watch silly things on TV, home is
where you play videogames in the background as I read, home is
where we dance to our favorite songs, home is always with you.
I love being able to call you home.

The Moon III

Tonight, the moon is a crescent, and it reminds me of when I was young, staring out the car window at the night sky, thinking the Moon was following me. This is true to a degree, as the Moon does follow us through life.

The Moon shone down on you the night of your birth and the Moon still shines for you today, bold and bright. The Moon has been with you through both joy and strife, for better or for worse, so say your thanks to the Moon tonight.

As the Earth Lies Still

As the Earth lies still, you lie awake, once again,
circadian rhythm nearly nonexistent, and listen to
the sounds of Night. You listen to the gentle hum

of the ancient ductwork delivering cool air to the bedroom,
you listen to the soft ticking of the clock you bought with Mum
at the estate sale in July, you listen to the ringing in your ears,

but the important thing is that you are listening to the sounds
of Night, under the white glow of the Moon. As the Earth lies still,
you lie awake, once again, this time thinking to yourself that it is
beautiful to be awake now, listening to the sounds of Night

in pure peace, in solidarity with the other souls astir.

Part III

Winter

Rainy Morning

It's raining this morning and my back aches,
the kind of pain that creaks and groans. I crack my neck
as I turn the volume up on my headphones,

boring holes into the wall across from me with my thousand yard
stare. I hum along to whatever is screaming in my ears, barely
noticing it. The rain falls and so does my spirit, the poor thing
stumbling along, trying desperately

to keep up, to not lose me completely. I try to be grateful as I think
that "this" is better than being engulfed in mania's blazing inferno,
but…how can one form of suffering be any better than another?
I turn my gaze to the raindrops outside,

the tears falling down my face keeping time with them.
I wipe my eyes with the back of my hand
on this rainy morning and scowl.

The First Snowfall of the Year

The first snowfall of the year is always an enchanting day.
I believe it brings luck. Welcoming in Winter and allowing it to
shake off its coat and warm its feet by the fire, the first snowfall

of the year is cleansing, signifying renewal and new beginnings.
As the soft white snow flurries around me, I stop and marvel at
nature's cold beauty, snowflakes landing on my lashes and nose.

I smile to myself, grateful to experience one of this world's many
joys in the form of frozen water droplets drifting down from the
clouds. I collect a flake on my palm and watch it melt, smiling
again.

Winter Solstice

Today marks the Winter Solstice, the darkest day of the year.
My mood seems to have reflected this somehow, as today
I have struggled immensely.

It was not just the shortness of the day, but more so the biting cold,
the kind of cold that you feel in your bones. I want nothing more
than to sit in the grass —

Shivering

As I sit here shivering in the December cold, staring
at the wall with unfocused eyes, existing solely in my thoughts,
drowning in them, more like, I want to curse Winter

and all it brings, but I shall not. Winter brings white powdery snow
that sits atop tree branches as if dusting them with icing sugar.
Winter brings a beautiful stillness, a forced stop, a reminder

to be mindful and to surround yourself with warmth and cheer.
Winter brings cold, yes, but Winter also brings yuletide
celebrations, togetherness, warm drinks, and cozy nights.

As I sit here shivering in the December cold,
I allow a smile.
Just one.

Christmas of '23

This Christmas I had to work, but at least I was up
early enough to watch the beautiful pink and orange sunrise.
This Christmas, I am thankful I am not manic, no gears revving

in my brain, no fire burning in my belly, no sinister voice
whispering in my ear. This Christmas, I was able to spend quality
time with my family and friends, laughing and smiling

with holiday cheer abound. This Christmas, I am thankful
most of all that I am here, sitting outside with a cup of coffee,
listening to the last of the birds chirping, content.

Christmas of '23 has been good to me
and I could not have asked for anything more.

Big Bright Windows

The Sun is shining on this winter morning, golden
rays filtering through the panes, glistening on glass
terrariums, providing warmth for the life they hold in
tiny ecosystems made of plants, moss and grass.

I watch the radiant beams dance and am without
a care in the world for how cold it is, as I am inside
under a warm blanket, covered in cats, no doubt
the coziest person in the whole world, green-eyed

beauties staring back at me with love, angels grey
who guide me. I rub my feet together like a cricket,
relishing in the moment of comfort, nothing astray,
all quiet as I watch the Sun's rays, a one way ticket

to winter happiness, all through my big bright windows.

Ray of Sun

As I sit on my cat-scratched grey couch this morning,
a ray of Sun filters through my accordian blinds and shines
on my face, warming me in its bright glow.

On this otherwise cold morning, I am thankful for this
small ray of Sun, a small token, a reminder, maybe,
that appreciating the little things, the things

in this life we take for granted, is what allows one to lead
a fulfilling life, one full of wonder and beauty. Thank you, ray
of Sun, for the reminder on this day.

An Ode to Plants

O, plants, how I envy thee so
placed in a window, doted upon
watered ever so carefully, leaves

shifted and pruned, loved and adored.
Sitting in the warmth of the Sun all day
would be a delight, a pleasure so immense

you cannot imagine. Green and purple and
yellow and pink, plants are diversity beautified,
conversation pieces, companions, hand-me-downs,

heirlooms even, as plants hold memories deep
and cherished in the hearts of many. Always growing,
always reaching towards the Sun, always up.

An Ode to the Sun

For most of my life, I lived in a dark place, devoid of warmth
and light. Each day shrouded by a blanket of grey, I let life pass
by in front of my eyes while I sat idle, letting time pass like grains

of sand in an hourglass while I tried my hardest to hold on to any
shred of joy I could find. I shivered and cursed and cried and wished
for the cold embrace of death, wanting with every fiber of my being

to disappear, allowing the darkness to swallow me whole, gone.
Then, a handful of summers ago, the grey clouds that hovered above
my head finally parted, and I got to meet the Sun for the first time.

The Sun opened my eyes to worlds of wonder and laughter and love.
He stood by my side even when the clouds threatened to return, when the
darkness inevitably came creeping back. The Sun gave me gifts

that are only heard of in fantasies, true love and an adoring family among
them. He taught me things that I will carry with me for the rest of my
life, virtues, truly, like patience, faith, and hope.

The Sun held my hand through my best and my worst, and for that I will
be forever thankful. As I stand here, in the warmth of the Sun's brilliant,
shining light, I am thankful with my entire being that I did not ever let
the darkness swallow me,

as I would not have had the chance to tell you
just how much I love you, my Sun, my forever.

New Year's Eve

In the new year, you'll find me trying to sit still more,
to rest more, to be more mindful, and to appreciate what I have
instead of yearning for more. In the new year, you'll find me

listening instead of talking, engaging instead of turning off,
slowing down instead of speeding up, and learning instead of
teaching. In the new year, you'll find me with my loved ones,

appreciating each moment and taking nothing for granted. In the
new year, you'll find me right where I am now, writing, most like.
In the new year, you'll find me as I am, and that's okay with me.

Dawn of the First Day

This year, I will —

Be more consistent at the gym like I always say I will,
but this time actually do it because I am worthy of a healthy
mind and body, respecting myself.

Get married to the love of my life in a faraway land,
surrounded by our families in a picturesque landscape
worthy of a thousand postcards.

Publish this book you are holding now, dear reader,
as it has been a life goal of mine to have my work eternalized
in paper and ink, held by curious eyes and hearts.

Appreciate the little things, be more mindful, and notice
the beauty in the everyday, the beauty of routine and stability,
of life's curious way. Mostly, this year I will seek out love and joy

and do my best to spread it too.

Flying South

I wish I could fly away for the winter as birds do, escaping
the cold and Darkness, heading towards the warmth of the Sun.
The lack of light and dreary weather do a number on the soul,

as humans are not meant to exist in such conditions. Winter can be
snowy and beautiful, but it is mostly dark and grey, a thick blanket
of cold that smothers the light. I wish I could fly away as birds do,

running from the Darkness that never lets up the chase,
nipping at my tail feathers as I soar over the trees.
It has not caught me yet, and I do not plan on letting it.

I'll continue towards the Sun.

Hummingbird

I am like a hummingbird, hardworking yet fragile, my wings never stop moving. If I stop moving, I will die. It is essential I keep my body in motion to combat the Darkness that lives behind my eyes.

I am brilliant, bold green, pink, white, and yellow, my beak sharp and pointed, ready to jab and stab.

I am like a hummingbird, sometimes flying too close to the Sun, always trying to escape the Darkness that looms from within.

Icarian bird, when will you rest?

Gag Reflex

Every morning when I take my meds, I gag
on the three small pills, tilting my head back
and choking them down. I don't know why my

body fights so much as I try to help my brain,
wiping tears from my eyes as I take another drink of water.
Every day on this Earth is a struggle to keep both

the Beast and mania at bay, the two sides of my proverbial
coin that fight for control over my life. I remind them, with
intention, that I am the sole captain of this ship,

and I will continue to choke down
whatever I must in order to keep them subdued.
Gag reflex or not, I will prevail.

Off / On

I sit on the couch and silently sob after working all day,
feet and back aching. I put on my headphones and blare music
into my skull, trying so hard to turn my brain off

for the half hour I have before I have to start getting ready
for my bartending shift. Tears roll down my face as I imagine
myself smiling at guests and pretending to care

about which gin they like while my feet throb and my head
pounds. I force my lips into a smile while taking a deep breath,
knowing that soon I will have to turn my brain and body back on. I
turn the shower knob and think

that at least working helps me run from the Beast, the one lurking
behind my eyes now, licking its maw and waiting to pounce while
I'm down. I have to keep moving I have to keep moving I have to
keep moving I have to keep moving I have to keep moving —

Roadkill

As we drive home from my future mother in law's house,
we pass a deer flattened on the left shoulder, eviscerated
by a semi, most likely. Entrails spilling

all over the highway, I wince as we fly by, speeding home
to our warm living room. I used to wish to be dead,
each and every day, praying to any god

who would listen to end my miserable fucking life. Ten years ago,
I would have looked at that dead deer with envy,
wishing it were me flattened on the side

of the interstate. Now, I wish that deer gets sent to a place,
an afterlife, filled with lush green fields, wildflowers,
and patches of clover, where the Sun never stops

shining and Winter never comes. I wish the same for myself.
I have braved the storm and I too wish
to live out my eternity in the Sun.

Dampened II

When there is no fire yet the ones you love
are still ringing alarm bells in your face, it can be jarring.
I am trying each and every day to walk the thin line

I am forced to walk between manic and depressed,
trying my best to find some sense of normal. It seems
as if every time I feel joy, I'm reminded of mania, of the raging

bonfire in my belly, the ugly feeling that rips and tears and
devours. Mania is not joy, mania is pain. Joy is light and it is a
beautiful, precious thing to be cherished, not feared.

I yearn to feel joy's warmth envelop me.
I do not yearn to burn up in manic flames,
reduced to ash and bone.

Tiger

It's as if I am a tiger, body full of spring-coiled muscle, tensed,
trapped in a cage that's so small I cannot even turn around
properly. My hulking body crowds the small space while my veins
pulsate and my skin hums with energy, like electricity,

lightning even. I show my teeth and give a most menacing growl,
but it is not enough. The rage I feel is enough to make one sick,
vile and hot and powerful, yearning. I cry silently on the inside,

as it would be foolish to show weakness in this state.
Alas, I am doomed to pace this earthly prison,
a creature confined, cold and claustrophobic.

Sinking

It feels like I am the captain of a sinking ship, an old wooden one
whose boards have splintered and whose mast is full of holes,
barely able to stay afloat even in the calmest of conditions.

Now, however, a storm batters the sea, wind howling and wailing,
rain the size of coins pelting your head, thunder booming and
lightning sizzling through the sky. You look upwards, towards
whatever deity must hate you, and curse this rotted vessel.

You resign yourself to trying to save the damn thing, as you don't
want to be remembered as the captain of a sinking ship. You yank
ropes and throw water overboard, trying desperately to reach

shore, willing it to happen. No shore in sight yet, you grit your
teeth and let out something between a scream and a growl, a
guttural noise

from deep within you, a defiant sound, willing yourself
to not stop. Wiping rain from your brow,
you set sail towards home.

The Pit

My depression continues to worsen in the chill of winter —
the lack of sunshine and warmth has really begun to take a toll on my brain. I am terrified of what is to come.

No matter where I hide or run, the Beast always finds me, teeth bared, bloodthirsty, cold, and evil. I know what it wants. It wants to drag me down into the Pit, the deep dark place in the recesses of my mind, a place where I have spent countless months,

years even,

over the course of my life. The Pit drains my life force and whispers sinister things in my ear, reminding me how worthless and terrible I am. The Pit means to kill me by my own hand, and when I was younger and less hardened, I almost let it.

As usual, I resolve to win this mental struggle, as I want to live.
I dig my heels into the ground as the Beast tightens its grip on my forearm, pulling with the strength of a thousand men.

I will not enter the Pit. I will not die.

On This Cold Sunday

On this cold Sunday, I want nothing more than to be horizontal, to lay in my bed and rot. Nothing I do seems to motivate or drive me, I want to be still, unmoving, and stare at the ceiling for eternity.

Of course I do not actually want these things, but my brain is making it so, creating a reality in which it may pull my strings, controlling me however it would like. I have to get dressed to go to lunch,

but even the thought of putting on my jeans seems monumental, let alone showering and brushing my teeth. It is maddening that my brain has this power over me on this cold Sunday, as it is my only day off for the next nine.

My fiancé is telling me we have to leave and I still have not put on my damn jeans, continuing my rotting. Maybe if I lay here long enough I will sink into the sheets, disappear for a while, just long enough for me to get some fucking rest.

On this cold Sunday, I want nothing more than to rot, but I will not. On this cold Sunday, I put on my jeans and walked out the door, now somewhat excited at the prospect of lunch.

On this cold Sunday, I won.

Rotten

Tonight, I cut a mango for my love that was spoiled
in the middle, brown and inedible. It seemed even too much
to cut away the bad parts to save the good,

so I threw it away and told him it was rotten.
I too feel like a rotten fruit as of late, colorful and bright
on the outside yet internally spoiled and decaying.

How long must I wear the mask? Must I play pretend? To what
end? Would it really be so bad if I were just rotten to the core?
Throw me away too, trash.

Something Soft

The Earth opens up to catch me after Dad knocks me down, yet again, embracing me in pillowy green, I smell wildflowers and feel the Sun on my face. I smile softly, knowing this is either a dream or that I'm dissociating again,

refusing to feel the blows from his fists on my back as he roars, louder and louder. I'm so tired of the dirt and grit, wiping blood from my mouth, spitting red on the kitchen floor, cursing him under my breath, promising myself I'll do whatever it takes to not let him win.

I will never be anything like him, I swear it.
The Earth opens up to catch me as I fall, head smacking the counter on the way to the linoleum. I'm sick of the dirt and grit,
I crave something soft.

I crave something soft.

Endure

My brother has started getting tattoos in honor of
each family member, and mine is next. For each
tattoo, he chooses both an image and a word

to depict a lesson each loved one has taught him.
For me, he chose the word "endure" and a peregrine falcon,
and I am beyond honored that he sees me this way.

I have endured a lot over the course of my time on this Earth,
but I believe that that is what has made my life so beautiful and full. To
endure is to remain steadfast, to hold true, to brave the storm,

to be a bulwark against bullshit. I am honored he has watched me endure
the dark, the difficult, and the scary. He has watched me endure the wrath
and rage of our father, he has watched me battle my mental health,

he has watched me both grow and endure,
and for that I am honored.

Sisyphus

Most days I feel like Sisyphus, damned to push
a giant boulder up a steep hill for eternity, never quite
reaching its apex. I am always pushing, pushing

through, pushing past, pushing my way through life.
I tire of the boulder, however. Its great weight always looms
overhead, threatening to crush me if I slip up or stop.

Sometimes, I wonder if it would be better to let the boulder flatten
me, to let it roll back down the hill over my broken and lifeless
body, blood-smeared and dirty. I haven't stopped pushing yet and I
have no plans to do so,

but sometimes it is nice to wonder about living in a world with less
weight.

Little Dead Pieces of Me

Tonight as I washed my hair in the shower,
I noticed that a lot of it had fallen out,
torn from the root like wilted plants,

little dead pieces of me stuck to my palms.
This made me feel sick to my stomach
with dread, like a rock in my belly.

Not because I'm afraid of losing my hair
or that I'm sick, but as I looked down
at the little dead pieces of me

in my hands, it reminded me of my own
mortality, which is the scariest thing of all.
Even though I am known to fantasize

about death on occasion,
I desperately want to live.
I need to see this through.

Smoke Break

I went to get some fresh air at work, needing a break.
I almost immediately regretted my decision due to the cold,
a biting cold that hits bone, the cold that sinks.

One of the teachers was outside smoking and I almost
asked for a cigarette. It has been two months since
I've had one and the temptation is still there,

the desire to feel the hot smoke cascade down into my lungs,
to feel the rush in my head, to feel the kind of calm that only
a cigarette can provide. But I resisted, instead offering a smile,

feeling the rush of a small victory instead.
It sometimes feels good to say no,
especially to yourself.

Crying Out

I want nothing more than to cry, but the tears won't seem to fall. They are trapped inside me, the Beast holding them hostage, not allowing me to feel the sweet release of a body-wracking sob.

Instead, I stare with unfocused eyes out at the trees, lost in the riling miasma of my thoughts, crying out in silence. "Just one tear?" I nearly beg, not knowing who I am asking.

I just want to feel real, to not just be the summation of these feelings and emotions that torment me so.
The Beast relishes in my suffering.

I do not want to fight today.
I just want to cry.

Groundhog Day

If you have never heard, there is an old Pennsylvania Dutch tale that says if a groundhog wakes up on the second of February and sees its shadow, six more weeks of winter are to be had.

This morning, scrolling, I came across a local news story — Punxsutawney Phil, our beloved groundhog, did not spot his shadow this morning. According to lore, an early spring nears!

Reading this, my heart swelled and my body seemed to relax. I cannot handle being trapped in six more weeks of endless grey monotony, six more weeks of bone chilling cold and dark skies, six more weeks of winter's bane.

I start to imagine opening all of the windows in my apartment, letting the cool breeze blow and allowing the sounds of the outside world into my space, hearing birds chirp and bright conversations, people rejoicing the fact we have survived another winter.

One Warm, Sunny Day

All I need to make it through this winter is one warm, sunny day, a day where everything falls into place, a day where nothing is astray, a day where I am able, for once, to feel the warmth of the Sun on my face.

All I need to make it through this winter is a reminder, a small one even, that there is good on this hellscape of an Earth, that there are good things to believe in, that not everything has to be shaded in grey, that clouds do not have to always loom overhead.

All I need to make it through this winter is affirmation that I am doing the right thing, that I am trying my damndest just to survive each day. Affirmation that all of this is for, I don't know…

something.

Family Dinner

I got my wish today, the very next day, one that was warm and sunny,
with skies as blue as the Caribbean, filled with puffy white clouds
and a buzz in the air, the kind that only happens on a day like

today.

I had to work but my spirits were high with the sun in the sky,
not a care in the world. Tonight we had dinner with my second family,
roasted pork loin, potatoes, carrots and slaw, bananas foster for dessert,

divine.

We booked flights to our wedding destination and I couldn't be happier,
imagining reading my vows to my love in a picturesque landscape,
surrounded by ones most dear, carving our love into the Universe
until the end of time, forever,

perfect.

I got my wish today, a day so warm and sunny it felt like Spring, full of
life, clear and bright. The Beast seems almost a bad dream, something
I conjured from the worst of my nightmares, quieted by the warmth
and light. With the Beast fast asleep, I am curious to see what comes

tomorrow.

Part IV

Spring

What Spring Might Bring

I want to be excited for what Spring might bring, but I am afraid.
I feel as though every time I get too excited about something,
the rug is pulled out from under me and I am sent falling.

I want to be excited for what Spring might bring, but I cannot
shake the feeling that the Beast will come for me in the night
when I least expect it, catching me with my guard down.

I want to be excited for what Spring might bring, but I am tired,
oh so tired. I am reaching my breaking point with Winter.
I need time to rest my soul, my bones, and my spirit.

I want to be excited for what Spring might bring, and so I will try
my hardest to be excited, truly, without shades of doubt
coloring my world. I want to be excited, so I will.

Icarus

It's sunny again today for the third day in a row, and yet I still feel
as though something bad is coming. The perpetual storm clouds
and the Beast should be returning soon, right? They must, or else

I fear I will suffer the fate of young Icarus, the boy who flew too
close to the Sun. Like his cousin Phaethon, Icarus ignored the warnings
of those around him and let emotion and feeling take over, caught

up in the joy and elation that everyone feels when the Sun shines.
But I am not everyone. I worry about being happy, catching myself
bopping my head to music or having "too good" of a morning

and wondering if the manic fire is brewing in my belly. The answer
is almost always no, as it is this morning, but it is still a cause of strife
in my life. Why shouldn't I be allowed to feel elated or overjoyed,

wrapped up in a precious moment in time where everything falls away
except for the warm glow of happiness? Maybe I can construct myself
stronger wings, not ones made of wax and feathers. I want to fly

under the Sun, not into it. I want to be able to feel that warm glow without
burning up, to feel that light without being blinded, to feel that elation
without fear of something coming. Is that too much to ask? Apparently so.

I look at the weather for the coming week and today is the last day
of sunshine for a while, anyways. I breathe a small sigh of relief
and pet the Beast who lays contently by my side now, like an old friend.

As hard as it is for me to accept, I am more comfortable while depressed,
a sad truth I have learned over the years and especially after I had my first
episode. I can navigate the grey landscape but I can't save myself from the fire.

O, Icarus, how I feel for you so.

Inked

There is something magical to me about ink, particularly black, but any color will do. I have adorned my body with tattoos, covering myself in eternal art, beautiful, sure, but each also a reminder that there are still things in this world that last forever.

I don't keep a journal but I do write, clearly, understanding the importance of words on paper — the word "spell" comes from somewhere, no? The magnitude of "forever" is not lost on me, as my "forever" is not forever in the grand scheme of things.

But, *my* forever is good enough for me, and so I cover myself in ink and write and write and write because I want to be remembered, I want to be someone who my loved ones tell stories about when I am dead and gone,

passing my memory down through generations, hoping to live up to the title of "ancestor," a beloved and bright member of the family tree. I want my existence to be inked on the fabric of the universe for all to see, bold and loud.

"He was a poet!" they will say, and I will smile.

Blue Skies

The sky is blue today and so am I, miserable
despite the relatively warm temperatures and clear weather.
I was desperately hoping an early Spring

would save me, but that thought seems comical now.
Blue skies and fifty degree days won't fix my
unbalanced brain, as my control system will always

be a bit off, no matter what I do. My therapist told me before
that healing is an uphill battle and, as usual, she was right.
I'm climbing uphill constantly, always

looking up towards the sky, wishing I could fly, far
far away from here where the skies are even more blue
and the temperatures are even warmer.

I know I just said that won't fix me, but I have to hope,
I have to dream, I have to wish for things to get better,
or else I'm condemning myself to death.

I can already feel the Beast salivating, tongue gliding over teeth,
waiting on the sidelines for me to give up, but I will not.
I will not lie down and die, but rather look

up at the sky and continue to wish, to hope, to dream
of better days where I don't have to work so hard just to live.
For now, though, I carry on.

My Green-Eyed Beauties

I woke up this morning with one of my cats on my chest,
the other beside the bed meowing, complaining about her breakfast.
I am so thankful for my green-eyed beauties, my grey and white angels

who keep me grounded. My cats shower me
with unconditional love, of course, but they also force me into
a routine, a healthy break from the chaos in my brain.

They comfort me when I am down, they lift my spirits on a bad day,
they make me belly laugh when they do something silly,
they guide me back to reality when I am off floating in the clouds.

My therapist recommended I get a cat a few years ago and it was
the best thing they have ever told me to do. Soon, one became two,
and now my apartment feels a little more full, a little more whole.

They told me that cats can act as rocks if you let them, that their weight
on you, literally and figuratively, is a reminder to slow down, to relish
in life's small moments of peace and joy. A reminder to be more mindful.

I am so thankful for my green-eyed beauties, my grey and white angels
who keep me grounded, beloved members of the family we have created
together. I never thought I would be a "cat person," yet here we are.

February

February feels like one perpetual Thursday afternoon,
so close yet so far, the shortest month of the year always
somehow, feeling like the longest. January felt like it lasted

years, but February feels neverending. February feels like
holding your breath under icy cold water, waiting for the moment
when you can finally come up for air, Winter choking the breath

from your lungs. February feels like a tease, with these warm days
and blue skies, knowing that tomorrow could bring snow and
biting wind. February feels like torture.

I desperately wish for flowers and rain.
I want to hear the birds sing.

The Moon IV

Tonight, the Moon is absent in the night sky, as it is new,
turning over a new leaf, a refresh for everyone. A new Moon
is a chance to start over, a chance for renewal, a chance for
spiritual rebirth.

I am happy for this chance, but I miss the Moon's light,
its soft white glow blanketing the dark stillness, not warm in the
literal sense, but most definitely warm nonetheless.

Tonight, the Moon is absent in the night sky,
just as the light seems absent in my soul. To put it gently,
I am struggling more than I ever have, desperately just trying to
stay afloat,

treading water at best. I try to remember that the Moon controls the
tides and She surely will not let me drown, but the sky is so dark
tonight without Her. I want to seize this chance for rebirth,
but I am lost.

What am I to do, O Moon?
When you are full once more,
please let your light guide me.

Blood In The Bathroom Sink

I know my depression is getting bad when there is blood
in the bathroom sink when I brush my teeth, grotesque evidence
that I haven't done it in a few days (a week?)

I know how bad that sounds, I do, but things like personal hygiene
fall by the wayside when every day is a struggle for survival.
I am fighting tooth and nail, literally, to keep my head above water,
to keep the Beast at bay, to keep the darkness

from swallowing me. Tonight, I washed the blood down the drain
with a scowl. There may have been blood in the bathroom sink,
but at least I brushed my teeth.

Our Little Red Café

We fall in love again at our little red café, the one down the street from our apartment with the good potatoes and black and white pancakes. We walk there hand in hand, rain lightly falling, the smell of Spring in the air,

spirits high, two hearts together. We sit across from each other, laughing at inside jokes, reminiscing on the other times we've been here over the years, rolling our eyes at the cheesy Valentine's Day decorations in the window.

We talk of everything and nothing at all, just happy to be together in our little red café, sharing this moment in time where everything falls away except us. The skies are grey today but I have not a care in the world.

King of Cups

On this Valentine's Day, I'll tell you my favorite love story, my own —

When I was sixteen, I went to New York to visit friends. Walking through Washington Square Park, I spotted a cardboard sign advertising tarot readings. I had never had my cards read before. Next to the sign was an old man in a blue wizard hat sprinkled with silver stars and a matching cape.

I sat down immediately. He asked me what kind
of reading I wanted, and being sixteen, I picked love. I wanted to know who my soulmate was fated to be. He pulled six cards, making a pyramid. At the top lay my soulmate card. He looked at me thoughtfully and said,

"This may or may not be a surprise to hear, but your soulmate is a man, a Pisces." The wizard of Washington Square Park pulled the King of Cups for the peak. This news rocked my world.

"How did he know?" I wondered silently, panicked, still deep in the closet, hiding who I was from the cruel world. He chuckled kindly looking at my worried face and said,

"Do not worry, child. He will love you like no other."
He was right of course. I met my love five years later, and he was everything he was fated to be, my sweet King of Cups, my soulmate, the one written in the stars.

Tolerance Break

I have decided to take a tolerance break from weed, as I am tired
of being dependent on a substance, any substance, to get me through
the day. I smoke to get by, as maintenance, not even to enjoy it.

I use weed to escape, to run away, to numb myself, to shield myself
from a world that wishes ill upon me, to quiet my brain that won't stop
thinking, thoughts upon thoughts of grey monotony,

to add some color to my life. Despite this, I want to be stronger than the
vice grip of vices, to live my life authentically instead of in a constant
green haze, to reach within myself to pull out some strength.

I need to show myself that I am stronger than the siren's song, that I
don't have to succumb to addiction, a weird thought for a former drug
addict. But I will lean into it, at least for now, so I can prove to myself

once again,

that I am capable of self-control. Who knows how long it will last —
I am hoping for at least three days. At this point, that seems like an
insurmountable challenge, but it is one I am willing to meet.

I have to. I cannot be chained to anything,
I am a bird that yearns to fly.

Down On My Luck

I must be down on my luck, if there is any luck to be had,
as it seems as if the world does not give a singular fuck that I am
struggling the way I am right now, kicking me while I'm down,
while I'm stuck

in this endless cycle of bad days. I have to double today,
and I would rather be doing literally anything else. As I flew home
from my first job, trying to give myself at least an hour before I
have to get ready

to do it all over again, I got pulled over for speeding.
I almost lost it in that moment, not believing my eyes, watching
other cars speed by, going way faster than I was. I must be down
on my luck,

as I said, as there is no way today could have possibly
been as bad as it was. With everything amuck, nothing going right,
I want to say that today could not possibly get any worse, but I am
afraid of

the world's idea of a sick joke, making it happen.
It would be just my luck, though, as things can always get worse.
With tears in my eyes, I brace myself for tonight, desperately
hoping I am wrong.

I must be down on my luck, that's all.

W(h)ine

On the first day of my tolerance break, I turned to drink,
refusing to be alone with my thoughts, needing something
to quiet them down. I bought a bottle of white wine the other day

that I intended to share with my love while we watched our favorite show
together. I didn't plan to drink the entire thing, but I did, of course,
my lack of self-control with substances on full display,

not satisfied with just a little buzz. I always want more, to be more numb,
to escape my brain even further. I'm a mean drunk though, just like my
dad, my words becoming his, venom and malice slip from my lips,

words that are sharp and meant to hurt. I cannot harm the ones I love
just so I can quiet my brain. I have to be stronger than that, more
resilient. I think I need to give up the drink for good, instead
of whining about wine.

Alcohol has never served me and it never will, something I must accept.
My relationship will always mean more to me than substances, as he
makes my heart sing and my soul warm, a once in a lifetime kind of love.

Struggling is not an excuse to lash out, to hurt
the ones you love, to use your words to cut and slice.
My battle is mine alone, but I need him by my side.

Pap's 82nd Birthday

We all got together at my aunt's house today for Pap's birthday, eighty two laps around the Sun. We laughed and remembered, told stories about times past and of things to come. New babies and dogs, new beginnings,

a reason for everyone to celebrate. Except Pap. While my family chatted away, passing around my new cousin and looking at old photos, Pap quietly said, "I'd be okay without another birthday."

I wanted so badly to hug him then, but I didn't, as this would have caused a scene, abnormal and out of place to show affection like that in my family. We are a family of individuals, loving from afar. But in that moment, I felt so close to Pap, as I too used to wish for my final birthday. No more celebration of life. No more life.

I know he just misses Gram. I do too. Our rock has been gone for some time now. I should call Pap more, I know, but I wouldn't know what to say. At least tell him I love him, seeing as there will be a final "I love you" someday.

Maybe Pap just wants to rest.
He has lived a very full life, after all.
Either way, I should have been brave and hugged him today.

The Siren's Song

My tolerance break lasted all of two days. I couldn't make three like I wanted. It's shameful to admit that I need weed to get by, to function, to feel any shred of joy in the world I live in, one shrouded in greyscale and shadow. In the darkness, when I heard the siren's song, I couldn't resist. It has been over a decade of depression and I am tired. I want a cheat code, I want a short cut, I want a magic wand, but instead I have weed. It is what it is, I suppose, but it still feels weak, somehow, to rely on substance to get by.

But is that really the word for it? Why should I shame myself for needing help, for needing a life boat in the grey sea, for needing a lantern to see through the fog? Why do I constantly have this desire to punish myself, to push myself further and further, to try to endure pain on purpose?

I need to let myself be helped. I deserve that.
So what if I answered the siren's song?
It was beautiful.

Dead of Night II

He sleeps while you lie awake again in the dead of night, staring at the ceiling and listening to the sounds coming through the cracked bedroom window, a cool breeze filtering through the room.

You go to the living room to write instead of tossing and turning, turning on the gold lamp, casting an orange glow on the walls, illuminating the room with warm light. The cool white light of the computer screen bathes your face,

its light reminding you of the moon, still absent in the sky. You think again how peaceful it is to be awake in the dead of night, while most of the world lies still, asleep, dreaming sweet dreams, hopefully. You know you will be tired tomorrow, but you are at peace.

Scars

One of my coworkers told me I looked miserable today, and they would be right. I try not to let people know that, though, to burden them with my pain, but my mask must have slipped when I wasn't paying attention.

I have intricately carved this mask over the years, one that hides all of the darkness behind my eyes, painted with a bright and cheery smile, of course. I wear it nearly all the time when I'm out.
I take it off when I'm alone.

I am tired of wearing this mask, however, I no longer care if people see the scars on my face and in my eyes, marks left from bouts with the Beast. I am proud of these scars, homages to my victories over my depression.

I will no longer feel shame in feeling misery, I will no longer be ashamed of my scars. Feelings are meant to be felt, not locked away and ignored. I am miserable today and that's okay,

as tomorrow will bring another day.

Tomorrow

Tomorrow brought me a day from Hell, a day that made me want to rip my hair out. Tomorrow brought me stress and anxiety, tomorrow brought me more work and less time, tomorrow brought me pain.

I am tired of waiting to see what tomorrow brings. I am tired of hoping on maybes. I am tired of wishing and wanting and praying, I am tired of crying and hurting and trying. I am tired, most of all, of tomorrow. I want to have a good day today.

Hope

I have the word "hope" tattooed on my left thigh in honor of my Gram, as she always wore a heart-shaped pendant with the word inscribed in its center, a constant reminder to look for the light, to look up towards the Sun, to not let life knock you down.

The concept of hope is difficult, as human beings are hardwired to only witness what is in front of our eyes, to believe what we can see, touch, taste, or hear. Hope is more finicky. Hope cannot be seen or touched or heard. Hope must be felt.

Hope demands more of us. Even though I carry hope with me every day, inked on my body for all to see, I seem to have lost it. I struggle to come up with any hope at all recently, despite my best efforts at summoning the emotion, that light, from deep within myself, from the very essence of my being, my soul.

It has gone dark, the lack of light most obvious in my eyes, devoid of any spark. That does not mean I have given up.
The Beast will not win. I will prevail, with or without hope, that flighty feeling that I will never stop searching for.

False Spring

There was snow on the ground this morning, a false Spring,
a gleeful little lie told by the Earth. Over a week of sunshine and
blue skies turned to teeth chattering cold and ice, the trees looking
barren and dead.

I knew this would happen, I knew it was not meant to last,
the proverbial rug ripped from under me once again, sent tumbling
down further into the depths of depression, further into the
darkness within me, freefalling.

Except, this time, I refuse to hit the ground with a thud, breath
knocked from my lungs, gasping for air and grasping at straws,
trying to get a hold on anything. No. Instead, I will spread my
wings and fly, dammit.

I have vowed to make friends with the Beast until I am rid
of it for good, if that is even possible. I will placate and medicate
and dedicate more time to healing, more time to tending and
mending and sending love to the Beast, my compatriot,

my cerebral Cerberus, my pal. As I have said, I am comfortable
existing while depressed, I have mapped out the grey landscape
that is my life, weaving my way through the obstacles and
roadblocks, a master.

A false Spring will not dissuade me from my path. I will keep on,
head down and teeth gritted if I must. I have worked too hard to let
a little cold and ice ruin me. I am an oak. My branches may bend,
but they do not break.

Birds of a Feather

This morning I watched a flock of birds make room for one more
on the suspension cable of the yellow bridge I drive across every
day. I awed to witness such a small moment of kindness in nature,

the kind of kindness that isn't thought about, the kind that isn't
performative, just done. Birds of a feather flock together, as the
flock is stronger than the individual. I am grateful to have found
my flock, my rocks, my support network of loved ones near

and far who are never too busy for me to lean on them,
to lend an ear, to show me the same kindness the birds did,
making space for me in this world.

Bloomed

No flowers have bloomed yet, but it still feels like Spring to me. Spring ushers in hope as the World wakes from its slumber, yawning and sighing life into the soil and air. Birds sing and souls sing, birds soar and hearts soar.

No flowers have bloomed yet, but it still feels like Spring to me. It is still cold out and the skies have been grey lately, but I have felt lighter, less tense, as if there is less weight on my shoulders, less of the Beast's claws and teeth.

No flowers have bloomed yet, but it still feels like Spring to me. The Sun still sets before dinnertime, but I am comfortable in the presence of the Moon. I am comfortable in this space between Winter and Spring, a tightrope walker.

No flowers have bloomed yet, but it feels as though I have. I have bloomed into something wonderful over these last few months, someone more resilient, stronger, seeing the beauty in small things, finding joy everywhere.

No flowers have bloomed yet, but I have. I feel it in my bones. I still struggle, of course, but my resolve remains unshaken, unbent, and unbroken. There will come a day when I'll be rid of the Beast. I know it.

For now, this is goodbye, dear reader.
I hope you have enjoyed growing with me.

www.ingramcontent.com/pod-product-compliance
Lightning Source LLC
La Vergne TN
LVHW041117150826
845673LV00007B/2092

* 9 7 9 8 2 1 8 3 8 0 1 3 7 *